UNITED STATES
SUPREME COURT
LIBRARY

Sandra Day O'Connor

by Paul J. Deegan

Published by Abdo & Daughters, 6535 Cecilia Circle, Edina, Minnesota 55439.

Copyright © 1992 by Abdo Consulting Group, Inc., Pentagon Tower, P.O. Box 36036, Minneapolis, Minnesota 55435. International copyrights reserved in all counties. No part of this book may be reproduced in any form without written permission from the publisher. Printed in the United States.

Photo credits: A/P Wide World Photos-cover, 5, 27
                  FPG International-31
                  UPI/Bettmann-9, 13, 23

Edited by: Bob Italia

Library of Congress Cataloging-in-Publication Data

Deegan, Paul J., 1937-
        Sandra Day O'Connor / written by Paul Deegan ; [edited by Bob Italia].
            p. cm. — (Supreme Court justices)
        Includes index.
        Summary: A career biography of Supreme Court Associate Justice Sandra Day
O'Connor.
        ISBN 1-56239-089-9
        1. O'Connor, Sandra Day, 1930-   —Juvenile literature. 2. Judges—United
States—Biography—Juvenile literature. [1. O'Connor, Sandra Day, 1930- . 2. Judges.
3. United States. Supreme Court—Biography.] I. Italia, Robert, 1955- . II. Title. III.
Series.
KF8745.O25D44 1992
347.73'2634—dc20
[B]
[347.3073534]
[B]
                                                                            92-13716
                                                                                 CIP
                                                                                  AC

Table of Contents

Page

4   Obscurity to Fame

7   From Arizona to the Nation's Capital

11 Reading Set the Tone for Success

15 No Jobs for a Woman

18 Her First Seat on the Bench

19 History in the Making

22 Appointment Made

25 In the National Spotlight

28 Standing Room Only

32 Hard to Predict

35 The Importance of Family

37 No Longer the "Woman Justice"

39 Glossary

40 Index

Obscurity to Fame

Sandra Day O'Connor grew up in the 1930s on an Arizona ranch miles from any neighbors. There were so few people in the remote area that obtaining a good education was a real problem. It seemed probable that only family and close friends would ever know of her in the years to come.

But flash ahead to September 25, 1981. On that day Sandra Day O'Connor became the 102nd person to take a seat on the United States Supreme Court. She is the first woman to sit on the nation's highest court.

Justice O'Connor and her family on the steps of the Supreme Court building, 1981.

The girl from Arizona had begun her journey to fame by leaving home at age six to attend school hundreds of miles away. Later she attended one of the nation's most respected universities. Then she went to law school. She married another lawyer, the son of a wealthy doctor. They returned to Arizona to live but chose a large city.

4

There Sandra worked and raised a family. She entered politics and then became a judge.

It was a productive and satisfying life, though one far removed from the ranch of her childhood. Then came a telephone call from Washington, D.C. As a result, people throughout the United States now recognize the name of Sandra Day O'Connor.

From Arizona to the Nation's Capital

Sandra Day O'Connor was born March 26th, 1930, in El Paso, Texas. Her mother's parents lived in El Paso. At the time, very few women practiced law. Sandra's mother and father, Harry and Ada Mae Day, probably didn't see a future lawyer when they held their first child.

As a youngster, Sandra knew a lot more about ranch hands than she did about lawyers. Until she was five years old, Sandra spent most of her time on the family ranch, the Lazy B. The ranch covers 170,000 acres on Arizona's southeastern border with New Mexico.

Sandra's grandfather was Henry Clay Day, known as H.C. He had founded the ranch some 50 years before Sandra was born. H.C. grew up in Vermont, but headed west when he was 21. He stopped in Wichita, Kansas, where he worked in lumber and real estate.

He saved a good sum of money. He used the money to buy land in Arizona and cattle to raise on the land.

The ranch's name came from the brand on those first cattle. The brand was a capital-letter B set on its side – a lazy B. H.C. moved his family to the desolate area in 1880. The nearest town – Duncan, Arizona – was 20 miles away. Sandra's father, Harry, was born on the ranch in 1898. Seeking a better education for his children, H.C. eventually took his family to the Los Angeles area. Harry Day finished high school in Pasadena, California. He decided to go north to Stanford University in Palo Alto, near San Francisco.

Sandra Day O'Connor (r) is shown on Easter 1940 at the family ranch. Her mother Ada Mae Day holds brother Alan, sister Ann is in the middle.

But Harry never got to Stanford. There were major financial problems at the ranch. Harry forgot about college and went to Arizona to try to save the ranch. He eventually did so with the help of a man named Willis Wilkey. Wilkey once had lived and worked in Duncan.

However, he too had wanted a better education for his children and moved to El Paso, Texas.

Harry Clay Day married Wilkey's daughter Ada Mae. They eloped to Las Cruces, New Mexico in 1927. They returned to live on the Arizona ranch. Three years later, Alice brought her new daughter, Sandra, the couple's first child, back to the ranch.

Reading Set the Tone for Success

At this time, most women did not go to college. However, Sandra's mother was a graduate of the University of Arizona. She even had gone to Europe when she was a teenager.

Ada Mae spent much time reading to her young daughter. Sandra learned to read when she was four. Her "storybooks" included an encyclopedia and the *National Geographic* magazine.

Sandra had no friends her own age because there were no neighbors. She followed her father around the ranch. She learned to brand cattle. She drove a tractor and shot a rifle.

At six, she went to El Paso to live with her grandparents during the school year. "We missed her terribly," her mother said. "But there was no other way for her to get a good education," a fact H.C. Day had recognized years earlier.

Her grandmother, Mamie Scott Wilkey, most influenced her life. Mamie was very supportive. "She would always tell me," Sandra said, "that I could do anything I wanted to do.

She was convinced of that, and it was very encouraging."

Mamie sent Sandra to the Radford School for Girls, a private school in El Paso. Sandra's grandfather, Willis, died when she was in the third grade. But she continued to live in El Paso with Mamie during the school year.

Sandra Day O'Connor receives an honorary law degree from the University of Minnesota, 1987. She received her law degree from Stanford in 1952.

Life now was less lonely at the ranch. A sister, Ann, had been born in 1938. A brother, Alan, was born a year later. So Sandra attended eighth grade at a school in Lordsburg, Arizona, about 20 miles from the ranch.

However, Sandra returned to El Paso the next year. Though only 12 years old, she went to Austin High School. Sandra graduated from the public high school when she was 16. She wanted to attend the college where her father had intended to enroll. She applied only to Stanford University and was accepted.

Sandra majored in economics. A Stanford roommate later recalled Sandra as shy, always calm, and fun-loving. Sandra graduated with high honors from Stanford University in 1950. By then she already had finished her first year at Stanford Law School.

Sandra became an editor on the *Stanford Law Review*. (Law Reviews publish articles about the law.) While working on an article, she met John Jay O'Connor III. Although two months older, John was a year behind her in law school. His father was a well-known San Francisco doctor. Sandra and John began dating regularly.

Sandra Day got her law degree in June 1952. She was third in her class at a time when only three percent of the nation's law students were women.

Some law schools, including Harvard, did not then admit women. One of the two men ahead of Sandra in her Stanford law class was William H. Rehnquist, the future Supreme Court Justice.

Six months after graduating from law school, Sandra married John O'Connor. The wedding was at the Lazy B ranch.

No Jobs for a Woman

*J*ohn O'Connor returned to Palo Alto to finish his last semester of law school. Sandra Day O'Connor looked for a job. She interviewed with law firms in San Francisco and Los Angeles. None, she said, "had ever hired a woman before as a lawyer, and they were not prepared to do so." One Los Angeles firm did offer her a job – as a legal secretary.

Sandra eventually found a job as a law clerk in the San Mateo (California) County Attorney's office. Soon she was promoted to a deputy county attorney. A year after leaving Stanford, Sandra left the county attorney's office. She went to West Germany with her husband, now a lawyer in the U.S. Army. While overseas, Sandra worked as a civilian lawyer for the Army. Two and one-half years later, John's Army term was done. He and Sandra spent three months skiing in the Austrian Alps before returning to the United States.

The O'Connors decided they wanted to live in Phoenix, Arizona. They bought an acre and a half of land in a north Phoenix neighborhood. Later they built a house on the land. Sandra and John both passed the Arizona bar exams so they could practice law in the state. John joined a Phoenix law firm and Sandra became a mother. Scott Hampton O'Connor was born October 8, 1957.

Soon Sandra and another young lawyer, Tom Tobin, opened an office in a Phoenix suburb. She worked mornings only. The O'Connors' second son, Brian, was born in January 1960. Sandra decided to quit work. John was doing well financially. Sandra wouldn't return to law for five years. In May 1962, another son, Jay, was born.

John and Sandra became active in the local Republican Party. In 1965, Sandra Day O'Connor decided to go back to work. However, she only wanted to work part-time. The Arizona attorney general's office hired her to represent the interests of state agencies at the state legislature.

In 1969 Sandra was appointed to the Arizona state Senate when a position became vacant. She was one of only two women in the Arizona Senate. A year later she ran for election to the position and won. She was re-elected in 1972. She also served as state co-chair of a committee to re-elect President Richard M. Nixon.

Sandra Day O'Connor was the Senate majority leader when the Arizona legislature opened its 1973 session. She was the first woman to serve as the majority leader of any state senate. The majority leader heads the effort to pass laws suggested by the leader's political party. O'Connor was a hard worker who "would overwhelm you with her knowledge."

Her First Seat on the Bench

O'Connor did not seek re-election to the Arizona Senate in 1974. Instead, she ran for a newly-created position on the Maricopa County Superior Court. Maricopa County is mostly the city of Phoenix. O'Connor easily won the election to the trial judge's position where she heard cases ranging from murder to divorce. She developed a reputation among lawyers as a demanding, humorless judge.

In November 1979, Arizona Governor Bruce Babbitt nominated O'Connor to fill a vacancy on the Arizona Court of Appeals. Her stern reputation accompanied her to the new job. "Totally cold" was one lawyer's appraisal. O'Connor wrote 32 published opinions as an appeals judge.

History in the Making

On June 17, 1981, 51-year-old Sandra Day O'Connor read a front page story in the *Arizona Republic*. The story said Associate Justice Potter Stewart was retiring from the United States Supreme Court. The story also said Arizona Senator Dennis DeConcini had suggested to President Ronald Reagan that he replace Stewart with Sandra Day O'Connor.

Senators often recommend people from their home states for federal court vacancies. Usually, that's all that happens.

However, in 1980 Reagan had made a campaign promise to appoint a woman to the Supreme Court. President Reagan had learned in April 1981 that Justice Stewart was going to retire. The President then had asked for a list of the nation's most respected women lawyers and judges.

Unknown to Sandra Day O'Connor, her name had topped the list. The President had then ordered the Justice Department to secretly investigate Sandra's background. The report had been favorable.

Eight days after Sandra saw her name mentioned in the Phoenix newspaper, the telephone call came. On the line was United States Attorney General William French Smith. He invited her to meet with him in Washington, D.C., to discuss the Supreme Court vacancy. Two days later, Smith's top aides were in Phoenix to interview her.

The Attorney General's staffers returned to Washington with positive reports. "She really made it easy," a staffer said. "She was the right age, had the right philosophy, the right combination of experience, the right political affiliation (Republican), the right backing."

Sandra was in Washington on June 30 to meet with Smith. On July 1, President Reagan decided on O'Connor as his choice to fill the Supreme Court vacancy.

An appointment to the United States Supreme Court is a great honor. But for Sandra Day O'Connor, the honor would mean a drastic change in her life. She would have to move from her beloved Arizona. She and John still had a part ownership in the family ranch. "Arizona," she said, had been "a land of opportunity and happiness."

Also, O'Connor would have to undergo hearings before a United States Senate committee. The United States Constitution says the Senate must consent to a Court appointment. The committee hearings can be an unpleasant experience. The nominee can face direct and even hostile questions.

Soon word leaked that President Reagan was seriously considering appointing O'Connor to the Court. She became the target of calls from reporters throughout the country. The possibility of having a woman named to the Supreme Court grabbed the nation's attention. O'Connor remained silent.

Appointment Made

Finally, President Reagan introduced Sandra Day O'Connor as his nominee for the court. At a July 7 press conference, Reagan said appointing a justice was an "awesome appointment." He said he wouldn't name a woman "merely to do so."

That, he said, would not be fair to women. He also said it would not be fair to future generations of all Americans whose lives are so deeply affected by decisions of the Court. "Rather," the President said, "I pledged (in 1980) to appoint a woman who meets the very high standards I demand of all court appointees."

O'Connor testifies at the confirmation hearings on her nomination to the Supreme Court.

O'Connor's nomination was not popular with many conservative Republicans. Most of them said O'Connor's record was too liberal.

Anti-abortion activists were strong Reagan backers. They opposed O'Connor's appointment. They were concerned with the moderate position O'Connor had taken on abortion while she was an Arizona senator.

O'Connor's appointment won approval from national women's organizations. And Senator Edward Kennedy, the liberal Democrat from Massachusetts, praised the nomination.

The confirmation the hearings before the Senate Judiciary Committee were scheduled to begin September 9. Sandra Day O'Connor wanted to be prepared. She hired a staff to provide the information needed to answer questions. She spent weeks studying recent Supreme Court decisions. She also reviewed material from confirmation hearings of other justices.

On September 1, O'Connor went to Washington to complete her preparation. She spent a couple days rehearsing the hearings with Justice Department officials.

When the hearings began, Sandra Day O'Connor was ready. She calmly answered questions and discussed her experiences even when her views came under criticism. The committee tried to get O'Connor to tell them her views on abortion. The Supreme Court's 1973 landmark *Roe vs. Wade* decision generally gave a woman the right to end her pregnancy if she so chose.

Abortion opponents want that decision reversed. But O'Connor refused to say how she might vote as an associate justice on this or any other issue.

The hearings did not change the opinion of those who opposed O'Connor's appointment. But the Senate Judiciary Committee was very impressed with the judge from Arizona. Seventeen of the 18 committee members voted to confirm O'Connor. Shortly thereafter the entire Senate confirmed her nomination. There were no opposing votes.

It was official. The 102nd member of the Supreme Court was Sandra Day O'Connor – the first woman justice!

Sandra Day O'Connor raises her hand to be sworn in as an associate justice by Chief Justice Warren Burger. Her husband, John O'Connor, holds two family Bibles for the swearing in.

Standing Room Only

Sandra Day O'Connor officially became the first female Supreme Court justice on September 25, 1981. It was a sunny day in Washington, D.C., and a very bright day in O'Connor's life.

There were two ceremonies that day. First, O'Connor was given the authority of her office at a private formal ceremony. This was held in the conference room in the Supreme Court Building.

President Ronald Reagan and Mrs. Reagan were on hand to watch O'Connor take her oath of office. Supreme Court Chief Justice Warren E. Burger administered the oath. Wearing a black judicial robe, the new associate justice placed her right hand on two O'Connor family Bibles held by her husband. She promised "to administer justice without respect to persons and do equal right to the poor and to the rich."

Also present at this ceremony were the eight justices already serving on the Court. So was the retiring Justice Stewart as well as Sandra's immediate family. The O'Connors' three sons, Brian, Jay, and Scott, were there. So were Sandra Day O'Connor's parents, Harry and Ada Mae Day.

In the afternoon there was a public ceremony in the courtroom of the Supreme Court. President Reagan returned to see Justice O'Connor formally seated on the Court. Five-hundred people had crowded into the 400-seat courtroom. Attorney General Smith gave Chief Justice Burger a document signed by the President. The document commissioned O'Connor as an associate justice.

Justice O'Connor then was escorted to a ceremonial chair. The chair was used by the nation's first Supreme Court chief justice, John Marshall. Chief Justice Burger called Justice O'Connor to the bench (the seats where the judges sit). Then she took another oath. This is the short oath taken by all federal officials.

The oath includes the words: "I do solemnly swear that I will support and defend the Constitution of the United States against all enemies…"

Then O'Connor took her seat on the bench. It was on the end, where the newest justice sits. Next to her was her former classmate and longtime friend, Associate Justice William H. Rehnquist. Chief Justice Burger welcomed her to the court. He wished her "a very long life and a happy career."

Three days later Sandra Day O'Connor was at work in her office in the Supreme Court Building.

Sandra Day O'Connor and her new associates.

Hard to Predict

*I*t is hard to predict
Sandra Day O'Connor's positions on issues that
come before the Supreme Court.

She faced her first major case in 1982. It
was a sex discrimination case. She wrote the
opinion as the court decided that, under the
United States Constitution, a school for
women in Mississippi could not reject a male
nursing student on the basis of his sex.

Some of her first decisions on the Court
involved the constitutional rights of prisoners.
She sided with a Court majority that limited
prisoners' access to the federal courts.

In 1983 the court decided a First
Amendment question. The issue was the
dividing line between government and orga-
nized religion. *Lynch vs. Donnelly* was called "the
most important ruling in some years"
on this issue.

The court ruled that a city could put up a religious display – a Nativity scene at Christmas time – without violating the First Amendment's ban on "respecting an establishment to religion." O'Connor voted with the court majority in the five-to-four decision. The decision shifted the Constitutional boundary in favor of religion.

Chief Justice Warren E. Burger wrote the majority opinion and O'Connor wrote a concurring opinion. (A concurring opinion supports the decision reached by the court, but reflects viewpoints not dealt with in the majority opinion.) O'Connor wrote that the Nativity scene didn't give "a message that the government intends to endorse ... Christian beliefs." The recognition of "a public holiday," she said, is not "understood to be an endorsement of religion."

Associate Justices William J. Brennan Jr., Thurgood Marshall, Harry A. Blackmun, and John Paul Stevens strongly disagreed with the decision.

In 1989 O'Connor was in the spotlight when the Court faced several abortion rights decisions. The most significant 1989 abortion case was *Webster vs. Reproductive Health Services*. This case questioned the Legality of a Missouri law. The law restricted the right to an abortion in several ways. If the entire law was upheld, much of the access to abortion granted by *Roe vs. Wade* would be removed.

The justices received thousands of letters from both sides of the abortion question. O'Connor got the most mail because she was considered the swing vote.

O'Connor did prove the deciding vote in a five-to-four decision upholding much of the Missouri law. Justice Scalia had urged the other justices to use this decision to overturn *Roe vs. Wade*. But they did not. Although O'Connor found the Missouri law constitutional, conservatives were still unhappy with her. This was because she did not condemn the 1973 landmark decision in the written opinion in *Webster*. She found state restrictions on abortion acceptable if they were not "unduly burdensome" to women who wanted an abortion.

The Importance of Family

When Sandra Day O'Connor was appointed to the Supreme Court, John O'Connor had a major decision to make. Would he move to Washington? The decision, he said, was easy. "Sandra and I have been married for 29 years. We want to continue to live together."

Sandra and John sold their Phoenix home. The house went on the market for $350,000. A swimming pool and guest house had been added to the original house. Filed personal financial data showed that the O'Connors were millionaires.

The O'Connors moved to the nation's capital. John O'Connor commutes between a job with a Washington law firm and his practice in Phoenix.

Almost everything had gone well for Sandra Day O'Connor. The family had the advantages of wealth and social prestige while living in Phoenix. Much of the family's recreation took place at the Paradise Valley Country Club. Sandra golfed and played tennis there. The O'Connors also skied together and once rafted down Idaho's Salmon River.

But in her late 50s, Sandra Day O'Connor had to deal with misfortune. At age 58, before the 1988 Supreme Court term, doctors found a cancerous breast tumor. She spent two weeks in Georgetown University Hospital for surgery and treatment. She resumed her normal activities after leaving the hospital.

A few months later, her mother died in the spring of 1989. On an April day, Sandra and her family scattered Ada Mae Day's ashes on a high point overlooking the Lazy B ranch. Sandra's father, Harry, had died at age 86 in 1984.

Sandra Day O'Connor's life got back on track later in 1989. In October Sandra and John's first grandchild was born. Courtney Day O'Connor is son Scott's daughter.

No Longer the "Woman Justice"

$\mathcal{U}$pon her appointment to the Court, Sandra Day O'Connor said in 1981 that she doubted that being a woman would "alone ... affect my decisions. I think the important thing about my appointment is not that I will decide cases as a woman, but that I am a woman who will get to decide cases."

More than a decade later, the big news is that a woman's presence on the nation's highest court is no longer news. Though O'Connor remains the only woman on the Supreme Court, she is not singled out as the "woman justice." Her opinions are presented as those of one of nine justices.

A century before O'Connor was named an Associate Justice, the Supreme Court had upheld Illinois' refusal to allow a woman to practice law. The United States Supreme Court had said in the 1870s that "...it belongs to men to make, apply, and execute the law."

Sandra Day O'Connor's elevation to the high court made that comment seem ridiculous. O'Connor is proof that not only can women excel in the practice of law, they also can sit in judgment at the highest level.

Glossary

Abortion: Expulsion of a human fetus during the first 12 weeks of gestation.

Constitution: The fundamental law of a state which guides and limits the use of power by the government.

Justice: The determination of rights according to the rules of law.

Law: A rule of conduct or action prescribed or formally recognized as binding or enforced by a ruling authority.

Legislature: The branch of government that is charged with such powers as making laws.

Majority: The group or political party whose votes are in excess of the remainder of the total.

Senate: A governing or lawmaking assembly. The Congress of the United States is the Senate and the House of Representatives.

United States Court of Appeals: A court hearing appeals from the decisions of lower courts.

United States Supreme Court: The highest court in the United States, which meets in Washington, D.C. It consists of eight associate justices and one chief justice.

Index

Abortion-22,26,33

Arizona Republic-19

Burger, Warren-28-30,33

Court of Appeals-18

DeConcini-19

Kennedy, Edward -24

O'Connor, John Jay -14-16,21,35

O'Connor, Sandra Day -4,6,7,11,12,16,19,21,
    22,24,26,28,29,32-37

Reagan, Ronald -19-22,24,28,29

Rehnquist, William -14,30

Roe vs. Wade-25,34

Senate Judiciary Committee-25,26

Senate-17,18

Stanford Law Review-14

Stanford University-8,12,15

United States Supreme Court-4,19,22,25,26,
    28,32,35-37

University of Arizona-11

DATE DUE			
MAY 1 9 2006			

921 OCONN

Deegan, Paul J., 1937-
Sandra Day O'Connor

GUMDROP BOOKS - Bethany, Missouri